Boy Am I

Boy Am I

Mark Cochrane

Wolsak and Wynn . Toronto

Copyright © Mark Cochrane 1995
All rights reserved

No part of this book may be reproduced or transmitted in any form, by any means, electronic or mechanical, without permission in writing from the publisher, except by a reviewer who may quote brief passages in a review.

Typeset in Bookman, printed in Canada by
The Coach House Printing Company, Toronto.

Front cover: "Ich schliesse meine Augen" (1993)
by Gideon L. Flitt, oil on linen, 68" x 44".
From the collection of Mr. John McCaig.
Author's photograph by Barbara Parkin.

The publishers gratefully acknowledge support by
The Canada Council, The Ontario Arts Council, and
The Ontario Publishing Centre.

Wolsak and Wynn Publishers Ltd.
Don Mills Post Office Box 316
Don Mills, Ontario, Canada, M3C 2S7

Canadian Cataloguing in Publication Data

Cochrane, Mark, 1965-
  Boy Am I

Poems.
ISBN 0-919897-47-9

1. Fatherhood - Poetry. I. Title.

PS8555.O35B6 1995   C811'.54   C95-932630-8
PR9199.3.C63B6 1995

for Barbara

ACKNOWLEDGEMENTS

Many of these poems are fictional, but I cannot remember which.

The epigraphs to the first & third sections occur in "I Sing the Body Electric." The epigraph to the second section is drawn from *Sheepish Beauty, Civilian Love*. Barbara Parkin annotated this collection through many drafts; the stanza of marginalia in "Cassandra" belongs to her, & appears on an early manuscript of that poem. "In Praise of the Masculine Form" alludes to Hélène Cixous's epigraph to her essay, "Sorties." The unattributed epigraph to "Latent," not exactly a quote, derives from Barbara Johnson's *The Critical Difference*. From Mary Daly & Naomi Foyle I learned to worry about the flying fetus.

"The Father at Twilight" is for Richard Harrison, who is my brother in this writing; his line in "Boy" is culled from *Hero of the Play*.

Versions of these poems have appeared in the following journals & anthologies: *Arc, The Capilano Review, Contemporary Verse 2, Grain, The Malahat Review, Matrix, The Moosehead Anthology, Poetry Canada Review, Prairie Fire, PRISM* international, & *The Wascana Review of Contemporary Poetry and Short Fiction*; & *Vintage 91: Prize-Winning Poems from the League of Canadian Poets, The Windhorse Reader: Choice Poems of '93, That Sign of Perfection: From Bandy Legs to Beer Legs*, & *Breathing Fire: Canada's New Poets*.

Robert Allen, Christopher Bracken, Mary Cameron, Wendy Phillips, Lisa Rouleau, Erin Soros, Sean Stewart, & Shannon Stewart offered readings, critiques, & needful advice. For these I thank them. Special thanks go to Cathy Stonehouse, for conversations, & to Richard & to Barbara, for as much guidance as a boy could desire.

CONTENTS

Impossible Lyrics for the Body

The Adventures of Kid Bean   11
Bowen Island   13
Glass   14
The Adventures of Kid Bean II   16
Killarney Lake   18
I prefer the talk of women (genetic text)   20
I prefer the talk of women (confessional)   22
Song of Kid Bean   23
Home: A Vow   24
The Bean is a Girl   26
Coming In, Coming Home   28
Circulation   29
day/care   30

Tonguage

No More Poems by Men   33
Snapshots : Thresholds   35
Cutting Promises   36
Mapplethorpe   37
Reunion   38
Cassandra   40
Cassandra Slight Return   42
Vanilla is a Flavour   43
Tonguage: 28th & Main   46

Boy Am I

In Praise of the Masculine Form   53
Craft in the Body   54
Latent   56
The Father at Twilight   58
Musk   60
The Tropic Body   61
Ursa Major   62
The Mission Ferry   63
Hide   64
Daddy is a Monkey   66
Boy   68

Impossible Lyrics for the Body

The love of the body of man or woman balks account, the body itself balks account ...

- Walt Whitman

THE ADVENTURES OF KID BEAN

I met you today, my child apparent
for the first time, on a tv screen.
Eight weeks & already in the media—

suspended beneath the great oblong
of her bladder
in the sac of your gestation

like the pilot of a Zeppelin.
Just under an inch
long, the size of a kidney

bean, one throbbing ... ellipse—
(forgive me if your present shape
sprouts a talk of spleen, but

embryos are polemical to me:
billboards, films, a fundamental
idiocy, the fanatic's prod

into ... the bellies of all women)
—& damn the evangelists for rattling
even a silly tribute. Really, damn

them. This technology is benign,
a hurtless eye beyond sound
& radiation, so you'll outgrow

an unwitting propaganda. This
was supposed to be a playful poem,
coy & fatherly, a trinket pun

on kidney bean, kid bean, get
it? child being? a burlesque
of exploits, amniotic swashbuckling—

you could have written it yourself.
But you are a cipher, saturate
with significance in a sea

of codes, murky to you & distant
as the dull report
of hammerheads butting the hull

of a bathysphere, buffered
by its own fullness.
Please do not be stirred

by this logos they put me through.
So long embroiled, my hothead
thinks this without me:

You are debatable: you beat,
the seed of a pulse, because your mother
so decrees. In the beginning, always

the speech act: around you, a battle
for authority, women's divinity,
the power to verbalize flesh.

March 1990

BOWEN ISLAND

See, lover, clover
stipples the suncliff

& thighs
serrated & black

comb sugar
from the leggy white

buds: bee & clover:
sex with the mirror.

—O she hums in the ear.
Tugs & booms

riffle the Sound. Rock,
lichened, leaves

us exposed
as petals, thinner than clipped

nails, rise to engage
a clutch of bees

knees / whose legs are
these? In a buzz passes

a floatplane's shadow:
seen love, clover, the sea.

GLASS

I wash *your* dishes now. The tumblers
chip, I never know when, notches
in the crystal lips, a shudder set
in motion when the flutes
tip. I am geared to catastrophe
these days, fragile as thin teeth.

At the recycling depot, a sledgehammer
pestles bottles
in the mortar of an oil barrel.
Hands grip the shaft, a man without
goggles, just glasses:
how tempered he has become to the sound
I wince at, the everyday shards
of a failure to cope
with the everyday. This shatter in my ears
is the rustle of flame
to a strawman, on pins & needles
in his own thatched shack.

We drop the hatch
back, & like an act
of forgiveness, the rear window
stays intact. We have grown
slippery with each other, as easily dropped
as words in a bucket.

I want to be sick. I want you to run
your fingers round
my wet, cracked lips. Harmonic.

Dusk. On the drive home, bugs shuck
their skeletal husks
against the windshield.
So many jars, so much wine,
the empties of a ripe
few months. This cheap cabin
with its round windows & deck
is a bauble now / to our unemployment.

We watch ourselves climb the step
in the picture window. Our bodies
reflect transparence, hologram
ghosts whose indulgences
are due. Within you, poverty lights
a hot womb, a globe that expands
on the end of a glassblower's pipe.

THE ADVENTURES OF KID BEAN II

I met you today, my child apparent
for the first time, on a tv screen.
Eight weeks, & already luminescent—

electron grey, suspended
from the oblong of her bladder
in the sac of your gestation

like the pilot of a Zeppelin.
Just under an inch
long, the size of a kidney

bean, one bopping ellipse
in a bath of salts
composed as the sea. We long for this

in flotation tanks, worlds
without argument. We rise, swell
into ourselves, suck fists & curl

our toes around drowsing, a perfect
& squirmy peace, rippled
with laughter, alpha/bet waves

that whisper no dispatch. We dream our parents'
palms, soft as lips, their gentle updraft
as we drift, cumuli, gaps

in the light, petals on the checkered
web of fields. We drive ourselves
with quiet inertia. The slightest

tip of the head & we shift
momenta, ripe with a weightless
potential, real & insensible

as helium. Yes, you can guide this vehicle
anywhere now. Harrow the gates
of Lakehurst, New Jersey. This technology

is inert, joyous, afloat over language
in a chill Atlantic sky; not a soul
burns anymore, you glide in mutinous

absolution, & the Führer's jilted voice
crackles on the wireless
into silence. The Bean is out of range

now but I see features, fingers
that threaten no signs, the chartless globe
of a tender head—unbound

& tangerine, the wash of dawn
streaked with vessels, trinket ships
to bob in the tub, your mother's steerage

& command. Rest now, wordless. When
you land, this medium will ease you warmly
into the cradle of our wet hands.

KILLARNEY LAKE

A plate of ice, grey as pewter, pocked
with the rocks they shotput from the shore
road, ripples with an elastic

mew, the quiver of a fiddled saw
or the sheet metal a stage hand shakes
clean of its thunder. These twinges

of sound bend downward into silence.
He pinches a shingle, clear as wet crystal
to spin like a frisbee. Every mosaic

shard syncopates this frictionless
mirror in the mountain's clavicle.
And he touches her face. The simulacra

evaporate. This is like nothing else
—four droplets on her cheek, glacial
in their fingered descent. Where was she

when he was twelve & a boy among boys,
every gesture a vandal's envy
of the cool perfection of glass? He

remembers now what he wanted from them:
this. In other boys a twelve-year-old
seeks lovers, learns desire in the queasy

rush of misdemeanors. To cast handfuls
of gravel at the stillness of things
then kiss on the mouth. To wade in gumboot

icebreakers, silting the pristine,
then kiss on the mouth. To exhilarate,
to get away with it, to conspire

in badness with one you love enough
to fear. Or to shuffle abreast,
a thin sheet beneath you, & to inch

toward some centre, some liquid depth,
where every touch is sharp, a lightening
crack that rises quick to the spine.

I PREFER THE TALK OF WOMEN (GENETIC TEXT)

I prefer the talk of women
when Barb & I at the grown-up birthday
are the only couple whose child is still due.

I prefer this talk of the body, its muddy insistence, hunger
for cheesecake & sleep, talk of dilation, six hours of pain
if you're lucky & We all survived it, Barb, we all survived;

talk of caregiving, an art like dance you cannot bluff
with technique. Of abdominal measurement & the accordion weeks,
heartbeats & gender, underwear broad & rippled as mainsails
& exercises to trim the womb. The way one of them laughs—
wisps of hair, misty tea—& breastfeeds on a bed's haven

or powders the raw crux of her boy's legs
& all the while encourages me, mock shy & she knows it,
awed at this surrender they survive, the inevitable body,
knowledgeable of itself, this resignation

to the blood, its welling & congelation, the tiny fission
within Barb that mushrooms us & everything beyond anything
I can harness, organize, manage like a resource or claim

unmans me, you might say, shears me (shortly) of language
& I listen. I prefer this talk of women about fathers
to the talk of fathers themselves. I prefer this quieter
advice: the reading, classes & the hard terrific ecstasy
of delivery—the way they can laugh about it

now. I prefer this fatalism to the tropic body I cannot
fathom. Mine would never do that to me, never swell up &
force its primordiality. The male body, for its championed or
lamentable force, is modest. It disappears in cycles, or

when I think it away, insubstantial as tissue. My desire
is stillborn within me if I choose, like the appetite for
tobacco, if you go without long enough, or the relish for
aggression, that other talk

in the other room of plastic Uzis for freeway shenanigans
L.A.-style, or rugby trips to New Orleans & being arrested
in the Denver airport, drunk at seven in the morning; or

deceiving customers down at the repair shop with a keychain
whose tiny chip feigns the chirp of a laser shot or testing
device ... or the slide whistle of a falling bomb. These men
love their children & their toys,

boats, these warmest excuses to bathe their hands in tubs,
slip down into their infant selves, with cellular phones
& skipping out on jury duty by pretending hatred for
the turbaned Sikhs; or embarrassed for me in my inadequacy
to spurt the neck of a pale ale in my fist

I PREFER THE TALK OF WOMEN (CONFESSIONAL)

until we realize it's not a twist-off. Yes, I condescend,

absolve myself, oh sure, *primordial*, I said, *tropic*, I said

oooo mudgoddess, oooo seagoddess, my *tropes* of anatomy *this altogether quite predictable return* (of the Same)—oh,

damn, I ply a shtick of difference: *How much gentler he is.*

But just another cock fight? I sought a certain *largesse*: the voice, expert on motherhood, soft & gruff from a purple plucky vein-bulging neck

in sensitive combat with other men, bigger & bigots &, Oh

damn, I prefer the talk of women when I am only a boy, eye-level in the kitchen & gaping at the true denim crotches & wallets of adults. My bowels twist & wring, dishtowels & diapers, *my*

inadequacy, I said, all eyes & sighs, eyes & economies, that anxious flesh shrivelled tight inside me, sea anemone jabbed by sticks in the cold Pacific society of fathers.

Every poem & politics: a contingency of fears.
Doubting John Thomas,
doubting John Hancock,
I mime a future, dance the lino
with rubber pants on my head
to engender envy in the other mothers;
utter oaths of involvement from the birthing room
ever after; I sing

a gibberish of promise & Barb yawns.

SONG OF KID BEAN

bop-bop   bop-bop   bop-bean-bop
bop

ba-ba-ba bean   bop bop
I be da bean
                        bop bop

—*I be I be I be I be*—

I-be-da-bean
bop bop

Ba Ba Ba Bean   bop bop

bop alpha bean
bop bop
        bo' beta bean
        bop bop
                b'omega bean
                bop bop

yeah,
bop.

HOME: A VOW

Four years
I imagined this:
your books, my books, our words
commingled as genes
in the cells of this house,
our first. Four years
like a monk in his coffin-bed
I composed myself with a readiness
that threatened not to come.
Four years, unforgiven, & now
out of the newspaper
come your plates, my steamer
in bamboo, the overlaid
wings of an oak table
& the fluke synchronicity
of dovetailing our lives
again.
        The way you plan
that fills me—when emptiness
is not my right, not right, this
onus, on you, to replenish us
with your relish
for herbage & legumes & theory
& a wooden boat for the bean
in your belly. Your will
to craft each day
generously enough
to hold a politics, cooking,
our writings & a child,
the salt of uncertainty
we lapped as cheaters
still on our skin. Honest
now, I love my fear of a desire
stronger than mine, mine
that would paint it all black, yours
a thirst for the world,
the antidote I never earned—

a rage to think & make & do
not think & pine & die,
that habit I nearly perfected
as a castaway, dream-certain
I would never find you
& determined to choose nothing
if not this unimaginable
return.
       I have rippled my chin
like an envious boy, killjoy
to myself foremost, have emptied
rooms with my manic
combustion. Physic, you temper
my soft hands with a rocker
& cradle, moving in
our sparse holdings
yet never so eager as now
to cruise junk shops & auctions,
never so eager as now
to clutch for purchase & pick.

At nightfall, the table
assembled, we attune ourselves
with tumblers of water, forks,
a lantern & three chairs:
the harmonics of a meal.
This time, we are choosing us
spoonful by spoonful, we are
sharing the speech of food
& making new lives
from nouns, from verbs, there is
this thing & this thing & this thing
we are zealots to just sit & talk about
for years.

THE BEAN IS A GIRL

Of course I never said otherwise.

But there was my fantasy
of an embryonic hero, swashbuckler—
the very rapiers
& biases of the tongue.

And the ultrasound
technologist
who defaulted to the generic,
that lie of grammar—
"his femur is two inches"—
then denied that *his* meant *boy*
or did not.

My asking eagerness.

Because I am a man
I am expected to wish my child one.

Guys, some other guys even
in the prenatal class,
snigger over a preference
they presume: bear down,
puff themselves
on delivering the Y
& congratulate
boys especially.

But the Bean & I are ambivalent.
She punches my cheeks
on coaxing now, my murmur
at the navel, tongue
along the whispery
cowlick that rides the swell
of her to the pubis. I take
a soft buffeting of limbs, moving
like rollers beneath the skin,
as she flies, arms high,
through her mother's coming.

•

Barbara is due anytime,
her every twinge
a flutter in my gut.
Barb is due, I am due,

I lied: We don't yet know
the sex of our child—

Taut between
this want of a boy
I did not need to be taught

& this want of a girl
  (to spite the wants of men
I teach myself

I am ready for anyone.

COMING IN, COMING HOME

her pain in the embrace
round my shoulders
when the head

emerges oblong
as eggplant
white with vernix

limbs slippery
in a sleeper
of cream

& when he squeals
out
in his hospital tuque

O
how her breasts
weep

•

On our pink sofa
we squint
into his pinched, red face.

With a braid of hair
she traces circles on his cheek
as he feeds.

I too have worn cynicism
like the greasy wetsuit
of a Channel swimmer.

Fingers, fine
as a sea anemone's, close
to clasp one of mine.

CIRCULATION

Radiators pulse & tick, pipes in the walls
a hot matrix. In bed we collect our threefold
flesh. But even here, fear of the body

grips me in a miser's fist. Rising then
after the midnight oil, a scientist
in the kitchen, I squander my health

into worry—the dailiness of washing,
change & exchange, dirty & clean, an economy
of care. Bottles boil & rattle, steam

the windows & dissolve the spectral
fingers of ice from the sills. Even
as a solitaire I never slept before morning,

but this year I am preparing
for the pre-dawn feeding of our son. In the yard
snow adapts its silence to everything,

wrapping each picnic-table slat
in a roundness. Summer sits frozen there.
But see how *this* season circulates its silver,

moonlight & streetlamp, from rooftop
to rooftop. The city invests its allowance
of light in reflection, a brighter world

where nothing is lost, where the value
of love, of housework, lies in currency
& repetition, the atoms of Caesar

that swirl with our breathing, the blood
in these chambers all living, as
another winter watches us through the night.

DAY/CARE

crystals & prisms in the kitchen window
bend bands of light red to violet
across a plump spectrum
of cheek
as devon sucks his fist squat
between the toaster & canisters
& i stir rice
with breast milk
into a clown-bottomed bowl

like all fool dogs
& writers our hearts flutter
with the flap
of mail through a slot in the door

& on fridays the woman in her truck
brings bottles of cow's milk
in a crate

after a nap & plowman's
lunch yolk & cheese
& yellow beans he stomps
in the jumper clodhopper
rumbles the ceiling
as i feed outfits
to a dryer that square-dances
in the basement

barbara's back
& the sun's moved:
we lie in hot patches
on the rug
play push-up
& blow raspberries
on three bellies
learning to crawl

Tonguage

The corrections rely too much on the body of the poem .... There are some things uncorrectable, except with the mouth.

—Erin Mouré

NO MORE POEMS BY MEN

No more poems by men
who showed great strength of character
in the birthing room.

No more poems by men
whose wives have called them feminist
& that's their proof.

No more poems by men
speaking for the survivors of abuse
or where men take the places of women
against the wall.

No more poems by men
in which the maternal body appears
as earth-like, ocean-like, vessel-like
or white as marble
or *dusky as his own lust*.

No more poems by men
who are fighting to keep the world safe
for a pro-sex attitude,
or poems
on guilt & the new warrior.

No more poems by men
sensitive on paper but creepy in person—
the ones who think
feminism is a career move.

No more poems by men
who are the victims of sexism, too.

And no more poems by men
who claim they have changed
in the past perfect.

(When I wrote this, you see,
I *had written*
many of these.)

No more poems by men, then,
that lay down rules for poetry.

No more poems by men
who pass off the languages of anger
onto their fathers
or the working class,
othering the blue
violence in men's necks.

No more poems by men
who believe they are not.

SNAPSHOTS : THRESHOLDS

I lurch to the curb in your ex-husband's muscle car. *Focus*, I chide myself, popping the clutch & stalling, neatly.

Inside, your girlfriend since childhood updates the collage of photographs she keeps butterflied under glass to reflect patterns in the lives around her. A memory board, pastiche of in-laws & coupled or uncoupled friends: a satellite map to her world, who she is, you are, today.

Your ex- survives revision in spaniel-eyed solos, dog-eared, overlapped or divorced by the scissors. Even our bald son, yours & mine, cheeses with his gums & grey-blue glassies, immaculate between his mother &, what is that?, a bowl of sour grapes.

Our unmarriage exiles me to the kitchen-floor clippings. Under-developed, a negative influence, ghost in the white margins but eavesdropping at shutters ... oh, I pose myself as a threat. Orbits full of conceits. I spy.

Smiling but exposed by my quiet arrival, your friend snaps —advances baby clothes & toys, an old Viewmaster, a montage of blessings to carry to the car, while I whir gratitude in hot shoes, flash you a look then drop to one knee, cartilaginous pop, to hoist a box near your feet through the doorway—

the aperture of your pupils swollen to frame ... a proposition?

I glance out: your husband's car, red as a magazine spread.

Will you be coming back in, then? your friend asks, wound up & eyewitness to a silence.

CUTTING PROMISES

Did you know the old Norse
chiselled their runes, prescriptions
from an oblique alphabet,
on the hilts of swords & drinking
horns, only to shave the figures off
in flecks over ales
they swallowed to the dregs? This
is a true story & testament
to the potency of the sign, its power
to sanctify by contact, the finger-
print of god.
               My epic concludes,
I love you for forgiving my return,
another little boy's odyssey
where *Thank you for taking me back*
is the ultimate obscenity & lie, &
*I would rather travel alone
than live guilty & grateful*
is the weakest self I own.

But again I am cutting promises
never to mince tongue with you
again. I am the man rubbing his wounds
with pumice stone: gore
to tincture a warlock's recipes
& potions for his own becoming.

So forget what those magicians taught us
about indeterminacy. Language
is indeed substantial, especially
when you have chosen to eat it.
Wait upon me now, weight
upon me, this is an oath:
I shall take back every public word
into my body. With these carvings & scrapings
I will make myself true.

MAPPLETHORPE

Paint my lips. Airbrush my jawbone with talcum, my
jawbone is shaven raw-blue. Blush me, rouge me,
feather my scrolled wings of hair. I say to my wife.
I say, make me over like Mapplethorpe, lips open &
vulnerable. I say, a man like one idea of a woman.
Make me that. Later let me preen in leather, tough,
the same angle, but for now I pout into your f-stop.
Don't stop. Do me like that, yeah, like Mapplethorpe.
Closer now, cheeks lavender & brows blue, garish as
our ancestors, faces of baboons. Come to me with eyes
lined, lashes black, your broad gorgeous shoulders,
your freckled muscular neck. Let a man & a woman kiss
a woman & a man. Two palettes, & smudge, pigments
& oils: a diptych. There is gender all over our faces,
mixed up & blended over all of our faces & boy, boy
am I, am I ever, boy am I ever in love.

REUNION

Bands of muscle   long & flanking
converge in the one well
of our hips   arched & swiveling
jointly.   Even now   after the baby
politics of everyday
spit-up & curdled
sleep   there are your eyes
as you flex   eyes
sharp above me & charged
with a power that does not threaten
& we are back in the woods
where we first made love
behind the Museum of Anthropology
to re-conceive the chances of women & men
together.   Touching my teeth
is the tongue   bittersweet with smoke
that never cursed me
in the birthing room.   Thank you
for that sharing
vice-clutch of pain
your whole body squeezed me through
counting down   nails
in my back   the tearful
release of our slippery child
between us.   Thank you for showing me
your giving forth.   With the tastes
of our bodies   now   mingle
scents of our baby   milk
& maple cookie   his essence
in our hair.   You see.   After all
this nucleus remains.   At the rise
of the pubis where we meet
this perfect pivot we make
we are identical.   Admit this
as a beginning.   We roll   exchange faces
& never uncouple.   Admit this
as a possibility.   Beneath us

sandstone falls away   runnelled
into gullies by rain
that finds the sea   its wet
fingers everywhere.   We clench
& unclench like hands
like jaws.   I exhale my entire life
into your ear.   You talk
back.   We are whispering
about our son   how he sleeps
elbows akimbo
the laconic teller
in an Old West stick-up.   We miss him
already   button in a hurry
to relieve the sitter who rented
High Noon.

    We must feel our way
down a forested trail.   On the nude
beach   where women in daylight
still fear to sunbathe
alone   a constellation of bonfires
guides us from the darkness
we are guided from the darkness
by network & semaphore   the crackle
& heat of other
lovers   co-parents   women
with women & men
with men in a jubilant
matrix of difference   the shadow
& flicker of flame that kisses
each angle of our various face.

CASSANDRA

You have watched me watching you
& disputed nothing. In my book
of our bodies
you yawn, a woman in dumb show,
O gaping void of voice—

the role I assigned you
by the laws of our polis
with the spit of my tongue
turning in the bed of your mouth.

Tell of your adolescence:
Turn around, your father urging,
amazed at the new hips
in your bikini in his living room,

your childhood his masterpiece
on reel-to-reel & Super 8.

So I polished my lenses *in turn.*
Born heir to the Eye, I accepted.

I projected
similitudes for your body
like a scientist
or a parent
believing he had created you
with his Word (6.0).

I am the father of graphic technologies.
This is my transcription.
All I have learned
was anticipated by your prophecy
but none of this is your fault.

A caress of my body on the page,
the record of that act,
is a quiet threat
to the autonomy of my living body.

Cassandra, will you speak?
Cassandra, have you been speaking?

CASSANDRA SLIGHT RETURN

The part of me made stupid by literature, the part
that compared the uterus to blown glass, full of hot air
& called it poetry (because it is!), is the part
I would disown, but cannot.

This is the poem that can only pronounce "I'm sorry"
in quotation marks.

(i am)

This is the book that says, *I take it all back.*

But there is no squirming out   body language:
                          from
                          under

(*Turn* & *trope* derive from the same root as *change.*

VANILLA IS A FLAVOUR

Orchid petals (dis)clothe
labia / in the (Jung)le
      les *tropiques*
pods of it dangle
like capsules of see-men
      / runs the r[he]t]oric.

From the Latin: a sheath, husk.
These cowls of etymology
conceal (him) & (s)mother her.

[Every poet (m.) with a teaspoonful
of theory
waxes parent(hetic)al
these days.

But conflation: the slender boyish bean
(in)visible within a name.

Which is it, vanilla? A probe
or a (she)ath?

                                                      (Search me.)

C'est/~~say~~ monkish for *scabbard*.

Left holding the (s)word.

& beating into ploughshares
is no help here.

Poetry Men
will figure
women as ships & ships as women;

woman as earth, soft-terra
vas-vessel;
man as
originary pilot-seed;
& the free-
floating fetus
as a cosmonaut, soldier, sailor
or person.

Men will ~~say~~, *I speak honestly
now of the body*

then anatomize
hers.

(S)hips, (s)oil, mat(t)er,
sheaths: vanilla is not
the opposite of S & M.

Vanilla is not *regular*, *ordinary*,
natural or *plain*. Vanilla
is a philosophy: bitter potatoes
mushrooms & bleach.

& I have hybridized old binaries.
I have gardened.
I may be pa(rdo)nned.

             (Guilty.)

Gardening: a shot in the dirt.
Language made me do it.
But I planted correctives. Fallow?

You see, when I use the term *matrix*
it's in the post-(blah blah blah)
sense, a grid of *différAnce*, etc.,

a geometry of growth, you might ~~say~~

44

&, oh yes,
it's a womb.

I have seeded & ceded
impossible lyrics for our bodies
because, you know, I love you

& cannot flatly ~~say~~ that in poem after poem.

(Chant de-natural liturgies
& just try not to Apolloguise.

(Get grounded, gardener,
in a process of error.

(Engage with your failures
till you get them right.

TONGUAGE: 28TH & MAIN

Nobody reaches me,[1] flurry
of inactivity. I am always busy

doing nothing; it takes forever.
Don't touch me: I'm thinking:

Intimacy
interferes w/ my work habits.

I achieve the perfect static
kinesis
of a racing cyclist
balanced to a stop.

Make your move.[2]

I achieve the perfect static
kinesis
of a gyroscope:

Back up, spin my wheels
around the block
just to avoid the invisible thread

of Ariadne-black-cat, the path of her rolling
eyes in my headlamp.

---

[1] I emulate the remoteness of the footnote.

[2] Or send photo w/ anatomical legend. Omnipriapic desiring, for obvious reasons, is incommensurate w/ life-long & monogamous co-parenting, Puritan. Or cf. note 12. Or kiss me, Charles Kinbote. Respond c/o Personals, P.O. Box, etcetera.

A black cat w/ white paws—
like rubber boots in the rain
to stay electrocution; white pads
to insulate the earth
from the body's bad luck.[3]

Nurse cells in the testicle[4]
protect the newborn sperm from
antibodies: a man's defenses
sense in his own sex, gametes,
enemies:
gender like a disease.[5]

The etymologies of *germ*.[5b]

---

[3] Because of a slipped disc, L5-S1, I am losing sensitivity in my privates, phosphorescent now from X-ray saturation.

[4] *Nova*: in this episode, conception w/ heroic volunteers—fibre optics up their urethras, fallopians, phallo/fallow/peons, cultivating a generation, generating ....

[5] Why not ~~say~~ something honest? I fear the body yet aspire to ... the Movement. The "F" in Kinesis. & self-reflexion, rubber hammer, Narcissus in a puddle of tongues. You know, ~~meaning~~ it. I (f)eel most slippery when I (sw)am most sincere.

[5b] According to contemporary psychoanalytic theories of paratextual notation these stanzas are underwritten by a pervasive "male hysteria" vis-a-vis lesbian separatism.

PAR	(by herself
THE	(Y is missing
NO	(MEN's land
GENE	(is a dead name
SIS	(dispenses with her brothers

Would it be xenophobic
I mean anti-French
to neologize
    tonguage?[6]

[7]Main Street, discount
centres, second-hand stores
junked to the doors:

Sorry, proprietor ~~says~~,
I got one but it's too far back—[8]

By the ton-
gauge.

& next door, the Immigration
Assistance Office:
lawyers in love
foray from Point Grey
to import nannies
from the Philippines.[9]

---

[6] This note (refers) only to itself, this note.

[7] Nexus to nothing, north to Expo. (The trope is cycling, remember, bicycling, I am touring the city, mimetic.)

[8] So the guy ~~says~~ to me. Or, the story goes. That is, I offered to purchase a night stand—for clockradio, plastic nipples, handgun, novels, retainers. We hate clutter.

[9] This is indignation? After the birth of our son we hired a housecleaner then forgot, exhausted, to tip her generously four days before Christmas. Why not ("~~say~~") something true? A: the barrier method: tropological slippage. *Hey asshole, vanilla is a* colour, *too.*

Proper rioters: Tongue cage.

Langwich sanduage.[10]

Tickled (é)Pong(u)e.

Ask a scientist: why
call them *nurse cells*?
Why not
slave labourers
in the ever-upward development of the phallocracy?[11]

Why not   Why not
discursive facilitators?   call Ariadne Tom?

discursive facilitators?
(A man
needs many hands
to hold his suffering together.[12]

Like a cat/fish needs a bisexual.[13]

---

[10] The poem nips out for lunch.

[11] Who elected those dicks?

[12] This is the honest part.

[13] There. Now I've said it.

Boy Am I

O my body! I dare not desert the likes of you in other men ...

— Walt Whitman

IN PRAISE OF THE MASCULINE FORM

> *Always the same metaphor...*
> - Hélène Cixous

You blue eyes, you ocean *tropicale*; you windjammer,
tight-butt ruddered, you full pectoral sails with flat
streamlined nipples to receive the air.

You germinator, oval incubatrix of spores; you loamy
crux of curls, onion-sour; you pink-pursed concave,
wrinkle-spoked, fecund & receptive as mud.

You trunk, teeming fir, steamy as the floor
of the rainforest; you lush limbs, harvest of mossy
hair, groundswell of muscle & blood.

Like the pillar of sand
a geoduck erects with its brine jets on the beach
do you rise or recede, chthonic & yet ocean-borne.

Oh let me squeeze your parts of clay like the god
that made you; you are supple to my sculpting desires.
You sea-earth-vessel flesh; you yield.

CRAFT IN THE BODY

You return to the game ice-cold
after nine years, & all is dreary:
air balls, fouls, jammed thumbs,
you could not buy a basket
or a decent assist. At six-foot-five
you cannot fail to rebound, but
nothing executes, your *gimme*
from two feet away
rattles around the rim
& jumps out, you catch
an elbow on the lip, split,
then pass to the other team
in a panic, till shame starts to sap
the blood of every shot
short.   But a moment comes,
you have resigned yourself
& fatigue's got you delirious,
faking it, a jogger running empty
laps of the court, when you
scoop in an alley-oop
along the end line,
take it down
totally without thinking,
& (stepping over a guard, his
planted knee) you circle
the ball around your hips,
charge beneath
& lay it up thru the backdoor,
the spin you put on the seams
squeaking the glass—

& that bite of the leather
is what does it, drives the wedged
orange, laterally, into the strings
& still you have not
even looked up, the guys all
laughing & slapping your shoulders, they
accuse you of holding back

until now, when the phantom
boy within you, his very lineaments
sketched in the strands
of your old neurons,
roused up
& spoke in the supple
language of his wrist & yours,
This is what we remember.

LATENT

Not difference between but difference within.

He is funny about locker rooms.

He cannot pretend a blind eye
to the beauty of clavicle, round pec, thick
forearm, or the gentle stretching way
a man towels his scrotum from underneath.

The heaviness of that flesh.   The *gravity*.

Sometimes his envy of the other man's body
becomes erotic to him. An *aching*.

& he cannot
not tell you this now, even knowing
you may use it against him.

But this is prologue.

•

He has ducked into the forest
the men stalk, south of Wreck Beach
& breathless, batting at moss
has patched together
dramas, hard liaisons, a community
from the details
of their condom wrappers.

He has nodded to men on the path
but not stopped, not turned his head.

He has conversed with red naked men on driftlogs
long uncircumcised
& exposed nothing,
peeled back nothing.

He has panted up the overgrown cliff
in his pants
wanting & wanting.

He has blushed & wilted in the proud
challenge to truth of their eyes.

•

Once he turned his head & cruised
by accident (this is what he has said).
He turned his head, twice, & led
a boomerang-jawed Francophone
in a green windbreaker
through the streets of Montréal

only to shake him on the escalators
of an underground mall.

Later he purchased magazines of the sort
he condemns when they depict women
in their parts.

The penis is different.

When he talks with women it is ridiculous.
When he talks with women it is dangerous.
When he talks with women he agrees.

But he is a worshipper. After the mall
he zipped safe into the Métro, tunneling its head,
its lambent slit bulb, forever into.

Now the man in the windbreaker
inhabits his sleep. He takes the man
into his mouth
beside his wife.

Even in dreams
he is tight inside his clothes, tight to bursting
from this life.

THE FATHER AT TWILIGHT

When the bullet rips the bristly side
of the day's third elk, slits the belly
crosswise like a knife, their father,

baggy-eyed, his belt looped with fat
& nostrils puffing, whoops in exultation
as its intestines pour into the snow

like a netful of fish, only red-hot.
The Cypress Hills spin in the beer-bottle
eyes of the quarry as it tumbles.

& the boys' father, seized in his glory,
falls to his knees, groin-deep in a drift,
to choke on the last hard spasms of his heart.

•

Always there is the problem of how
to collect the kill. By the time the boys
can lash the hooves of the first elk,

shoulder the pole half a mile
to the truck & rack up the rifles,
the sky is hemorrhaging to purple.

They return to the body of their father,
his eyeballs milky & lidless
even under the pressure of a thumb.

The first lesson was never to waste
good meat, but the second elk, a bull,
is too heavy for two & must be left.

The third, its guts dangling
over the snow, measling their bootprints,
they nestle into the truckbed beside the first.

•

At dusk the body of the patriarch, abundant
flesh & unbending hips, cannot be borne
with the lashes & staff.

The evergreens are cassocks, observant
silhouettes, as the boys drag the stiff
burden of their father across

silence in the snowy fields, his
ankles in their mitts, wide buttocks
shovelling a furrow, his head

in its tuque, pillowed by a dead arm
& sliding. Against the truck they balance
him erect, contemplate the cab, its

S-curve of vinyl seats & the unfitting
shape of the door. Against this dilemma
they talk of the cold, a night of driving,

their mother & the uncle who cleans
carcasses. Beneath a tarp, between his prey,
new men must prepare a place for the Father.

MUSK

sweat sharper
than the whole-body sweat.
the smell I remember
of my uncle, his sex
& coffee & tobacco
at breakfast, breathing through
the richness of his fingers
on the farm where he died a bachelor.

smell on my hands, I drink it in,
absorption to the gelatinous
buds of my lungs
a replenishment
of what I am

this taint that remains
epidermal
from a night's cupping
& soaked cell-deep
even after I shower.

the smell also, gamy & piquant,
akin to mine
& yet distinct,
of unsoaped men who sleep
clothed in the streets downtown

: fetal & palming
heat from the pocket of the groin.

THE TROPIC BODY

i love this
morning, tide of sleep,
tropic flush
of the whole body
i wash in touch
long hollow
strand of ribs
& pale nipples
vestigial or equivocal
whorled with hair
funnels past
the gaping Om-
phalos to the night's
engorgement, split
column, spongy
bladders of blood
nubbinned with scar
tissue, the cock's
centre seam
fingers follow
to a pouch bathing
(orchid, *orchis*, bulb)
loose & tubules
coiled in a sac,
underside
smooth but ridged,
this thin raphe
or radius to the anus
the same seam
that sealed
(so i say)
when the catholic
fe/male
fetus that i was
became a boy,
aquatic.

URSA MAJOR

That evening, after the bear had shaken itself free of the rainforest & raided their cache on the seashore at dawn, sucking bacon, Bugles, hamburger & buns from the cooler,

the boy was hunching over his presexual body, hairless beluga in a motel-room bathtub, his father above him shaving at the sink before dinner,

when in the water a beetle manifested larger than a Brazil nut, its clear-brown shell & sawtooth limbs prickling the smooth of the boy's thigh.

What he remembers of his father as a young man is a thick paw whose touch was tender as a woman's hand. What he remembers are bear hugs, even as he grew bulky & awkward.

But when he yelped, scooping up water around the insect & sogging the bathmat, his father turned, great cock arched over the foam flecked with whiskers, turned his broad skull, scowl, & grumbled from deep in the furze of his torso.

That night, in the boy's dream, a form loomed by the mirror pool, a white drool falling from its lips like the unction to transform his distilled skin.

That morning, when a bear strafed their campsite on Long Beach, it had risen tall against a canopy of stars. It had peered, placid & quizzical, into a tidal basin: past the ripple of its reflection, & through the watery glint of constellations, to an anemone, sunken inside itself like the genitals of a child.

THE MISSION FERRY

Everything is used up, the thrush
hits the picture window, it's
broken inside, its
head out of joint, its
pincushion body of snapped bones
in the shoebox. There is no soil
we have not squeezed thru our fingers,
the water in this river
has been used before, even in this country
nothing is itself, the freeway crazy with
a car pulling a car
on a trailer, fishtailing, into the ditch
right in front, we could have died,
our son in his carseat
or you, running along the median
for help, at the convenience store, exit
73, alerting the RCMP then waiting
for a ferry
to cross the river to Mission,
river of water that has been used before,
passed thru bodies & leached thru culverts
under roads
to the SPCA,
water that suspends a ferry of cars
above the sludge,
the black unlivable sludge
with a broken thrush in a shoebox
on the seat beside our son, its rustle
in that darkness as we rush, we rush.

HIDE

There is a man who holds himself together. Elephant skin.
He contracts himself like a raisin. Or like elephant skin.
Thick & wrinkled he tightens his leathery mail, his ridges
& ripples. His plies enfold. Shoulder pads. He holds all
his secrets inside him. Tough mammal, paresthetic. Numb
shield, sclerotic. Mammoth grey, batik skin. Waxy cracked
& cracked & cracked.

•

Once upon a time he surrendered. Once upon a time the man
just let go. He relaxed & every riven surface of his sad
body, epidermic periphery, sundered like a scab, it did, &
weepy, as yellowish plasma it was stringy & wept. Viscous.
Agglutinate. He opened wide, his eyes to see, & his crow's
feet peeled back, slit.

•

When he is not holding tight, tragedy. Accidents happen
at non-random intervals by this interface. From behind him
there is a certain wailing or, screeching. He stretched out
& the skin on his arms split like desert earth, like dried
icing on a cake, like a thin sheen of plaster of Paris.
It split like Job.

•

His burst lids. Pupils from side to side. He opened to
relish & became witness to the one truth, loss. When this
happens there is no place he can go, that is not thinking.
Or move without tearing. He crackles, he pops inside his
clothes. Fabric clots in the wounds. Accidents are not.

•

There is a man who is driving to Emergency. Knuckle hide
on the steering wheel rends slowly, cell by elongated cell,
like a pink eraser. The auto is slippery with the fluids
of humans losing a certain wholeness.

•

Only a parent can understand what I am about to say. Only
givers of such care. The dashboard is smeared, the seat
is tacky. A certain redness lies about. Once upon a time
a man relaxed with his child & an accident happened
at a precise & non-random interval. The man stretched
in the blanched winter sun with fate, who is his child, &
speed & force were the functions of ice.

Crack.

•

He tightens, no, he shrinks inside the skin of his grip.

DADDY IS A MONKEY

quips my son, gap-toothed
from his fall on the ice, a whole person
glistering from his eyes
to mine, hiccuping

giggles at his own joke,
just two-&-a-half
with a toy chimp stuffed
into a helmet & jersey
& playing in the slot

between his grandpa—my father—& me
on the sofa, as we dangle
from the final seconds
of the Kings' game, an arena
where we can meet, Dad reaching out
across space
& *his* father's pocket-watch, arranged
like a trophy on the hutch,
to caress my arm—

an awkward
animal grooming
in the glade of his apartment,
neither of us possessing
speech for this—

his opposable thumb in the hair
above my wrist
where the blood warms,
soothed & confused by the same touch
that tended me
when i was the boy who loved him
full in the face,
as a child will allow
for only so long: full
& unmasked, without a helmet
painted with a crown, & free
from the dread of any loss, sudden
or slow, even
as the clock was running down.

BOY

Cathy says
*You are always using the word
but I wonder what it means for you.*

Richard says
This is my hockey. Did you ever see me play it?

I say
I hate the Father, but I love my dad.

•

Desperate for something but relieved at nothing
I bowed my head, I waited & waited
for a crop of hair, dark nimbus
to appear
& blot the white
chub of the pubis.

It was the one page I could not write, by will.

At twelve I quit the city "A" league
when smaller boys
with their compact torsion
began to lay me flat. I was big
but soft, sweat not pungent, not yet musk,
& worst of all
I was glad for that.

Trace to this moment, if you must,
my fear of shower-rooms & locker chat.

O pupae, O the smooth & featureless.
Grown men, the emissions of their skins,
revulsed me, & like (& unlike) a girl too thin
& wanting to be thinner, breastless, I dreaded
metamorphosis.

Every story of the adulthood of my body
begins the year I quit hockey clean, without muscle, &

when puberty finally came, I was fourteen,
it was too late. Manhood already knew
I was a traitor to its form.

But desire doubles back on disgust.
Now I'm back in the game with other men
& can hardly tell repulsion, or jealousy, from lust.

The homoerotic? I consume the other man in mind
to become him, sculpted & buffed
to a sheen, my ideal self in the imagined
eyes of women. (Oh, that's one disavowal ...

O Daddy, O Daedalus, O magician:
because I could never measure up to your body
or your idea of it, brute & heavy
but perfectible, tight, & sexed for flight,

because I could never harden myself
to the sleekness of a rooster & rise,

I nearly drowned in a refusal
of the wings you had invented, I nearly proved
that the impressionable son
melts.

•

My dad, in the autumn of his seventeenth year,
was on the cusp of making
the major-junior team in Moose Jaw

(& everything that promised)

when he took a football cleat in the calf
& lost the season of both sports.

Where I come from
athletics are a man's first career.
Any other life
is a rebellion or a compromise
based on the failure to make pro.

Yesterday in the community centre
I stepped onto the rink, ice
wet & bluish
like the white of an eye
after the Zamboni run.

That smell, *air of the ice*, it hit me
like a shoulder to the lungs:

I am six years old & taking a face-off

at five-thirty in the morning, my dad
is a bushy bear
with seventies hair
& his moustache in the steam—

he is smiling over coffee—

a warm
rush of reassurance
from his cupped hands of prayer
in the stands.

•

This spring, after many apart, we attend
NHL games
like devotions, the arcana
& arithmetic of the sportspage
a way of talking.

As fathers, as dads, we are beginning
to find a way back, through men & their measures,
to the meaning of a boy
& the soft, muscular care
he was born to.